MW01504390

Race Fans' Devotions to Go

Encouragement for Your Day-to-Day Race of Life

Beth Bence Reinke

Lonna —
Blessings in your
"race of life!" :)
Beth Bence Reinke
2013

The devotions in Race Fans' Devotions to Go are based on the author's personal experiences and observations. This book, its author and publisher are not officially endorsed by or affiliated with the National Association of Stock Car Auto Racing or any racing-related organizations, teams, drivers or other personnel.

Copyright Beth Bence Reinke, 2012

All Rights Reserved

Published by See Media, Inc.

Carson City, NV

ISBN: 978-1-934626-29-0

Printed in the United States of America

Acknowledgments

The author wishes to thank the following people for their kind assistance during the creation of this book: Gary Camp, Jean Ann Duckworth, Benny Gordon, Billy Mauldin, KimberLee Mudge, Rosalie Nestore, Patrick Perkins, Pattie Petty, Sallie Randolph, Frank Rossi, Elia Trowbridge, and Mary Vaughn.

Race Fans' Devotions to Go

Race Fans' Devotions to Go

Introduction

Dear friend,

Does your heart speed up in anticipation of the green flag? Then this book was written just for you. Whether you sit in the grandstand or watch on television, there is nothing as thrilling to a race fan as stock car engines revving up for a race.

These devotions illustrate parallels between racing and our real lives as women. At the end of each devotion is a "pit stop" – an idea for a minor adjustment to make your life better or easier. I hope you will be encouraged by the practical, biblical advice in these pages and gain a fresh perspective on the sport we love.

My fellow NASCAR fan, I invite you to put on your favorite driver cap and buckle up. It's time for some racing!

Blessings,
Beth

P.S. Throughout this book, masculine pronouns are used in reference to drivers only for purposes of simplicity. No slight to the up-and-coming female drivers is intended. In fact, I'm thrilled to see women competing at the highest levels of racing - go ladies!

Race Fans' Devotions to Go

#1
Splash-and-Go to Your Goals

For God did not give us a spirit of timidity,
but a spirit of power, of love and of self-discipline.
2 Timothy 1:7

Imagine your favorite driver is leading a race with two laps to go. As he rounds turn four, your heart is pounding, anticipating the white flag. Suddenly competitors zoom by on both sides and he appears to be sliding backwards. Your driver coasts toward the apron and rolls to a stop. Oh no, he's out of gas!

No one likes running out of gas at the end and not being able to cross the finish line. Sometimes it happens due to miscalculations on fuel mileage. Sometimes staying out to keep track position backfires because of extra laps from multiple green-and-white checkered flags.

Drivers who know they might be short on fuel are thrilled when a late caution allows them to splash-and-go, especially if most of the field pits. That little bit of gasoline means they can make it to the end.

When high speed is the goal, fuel mileage racing seems counter-intuitive. Think how difficult it must be for a guy to save fuel when his natural inclination is "hammer down" racing -- go, go, go!

It takes tremendous, grit-your-teeth self-discipline to hold back in order to squeeze the most distance out of every drop in the tank. A driver must keep a steady foot because pumping the accelerator uses more gas. If he has enough of a lead, he might let up on the gas and coast, keeping an eye on the rearview mirror. If more than one of the leaders are short on fuel, the guy who is the most self-disciplined at conserving might end up in Victory Lane.

Self-discipline? Ugh. We groan and roll our eyes at the notion of it, like it's a horrible, pain-staking thing we have to do. But being disciplined can lead to incredible benefits - like winning a race or fitting into skinny jeans or saving money for a family vacation.

Perhaps we should reverse the way we think about self-discipline. Instead of whining about self-deprivation, let's think of discipline as cultivating a good habit that makes your life better. Need some examples? 1) Your driver's goal is to save fuel. Instead of depriving himself of full-throttle racing, he gives himself the gift of finishing the race. 2) Let's say your goal is to eat healthy. Instead of depriving yourself of cookies, you give yourself the gift of fresh fruit. 3) Your goal is to de-clutter your house. Instead of forcing yourself to rid up a room, give yourself the gift of a tidy space. Get the idea?

Identify an area of your life where you yearn for more self-discipline. Refuse to talk about your goal in terms of depriving yourself. Instead, think of it as nurturing a positive habit that will bless you in the long run. What gift will you give yourself today?

Prayer: Dear God, I truly want to pursue a constructive habit without feeling deprived or punished. Please help me to rely on your strength and to focus on the blessings that come with meeting my goals. In Jesus' name, Amen.

Pit Stop

We have redefined self-discipline as "cultivating a good habit that makes your life better." Whether you're trying to quit smoking, spend less or exercise more, remember that your goal is to give yourself a gift by engaging in a new, good habit.

When you plant a garden, you need to prepare ahead so the seeds you cultivate will grow - turn over the soil, add fertilizer, toss out rocks and weeds. A little planning helps with self-discipline, too. Preparations are like a splash-and-go stop that helps you make it to the checkered flag with your new habit.

What kinds of things can you do? If you want to slash sugar intake, rid your cupboards of sweet treats. If you wish to decrease spending, cut up the credit card. To exercise more, get out your workout DVD and hand weights and sit them by the television. Do little things ahead of time that will help you to succeed.

To spur you on, print out this encouraging verse on pretty paper in big letters and post it where you need it:

I can do everything through him who gives me strength. Philippians 4:13

#2
The Heavenly Spotter

*But the Counselor, the Holy Spirit, whom the Father will
send in my name,
will teach you all things and will remind you of everything I
have said to you.*
John 14:26

Each driver has one team member who is not on pit road or in the garage. The spotter is the driver's "eye in the sky." From his vantage point on top of the grandstands or above the press box, the spotter has a unique perspective on the race. He spots things happening on the track that the crew chief and even the driver himself may not observe.

The spotter has direct radio communication with the driver, giving him essential information no one else can provide. If there is a crash on the track, the spotter tells the driver where to go to avoid getting caught up in it. You might hear a spotter exclaim, "Go high!" when cars are wrecking down near the apron. Oftentimes the driver can't see through the thick smoke enveloping the accident. But from his high perch, the spotter has a better view and guides his driver safely through the gray haze into the clear.

If you're a Christian, help from high places is available to you, too – from the Holy Spirit. In racing terms, we might think of the Holy Spirit as a "Heavenly Spotter." The Holy Spirit has a heavenly vantage point and perceives things in our lives we cannot see. He stays with you throughout your life just like a spotter sticks with a driver for the whole race. Jesus told his disciples that the Holy Spirit would come to stay with them as a constant helper and teacher.

When I was nine years old and learned about Jesus, I didn't understand this. I heard the name "Holy Spirit" or "Holy Ghost" in church services and recognized that God had three parts: the Father (God), the Son (Jesus) and the Holy Spirit. But I did not know where the Holy Spirit was or what He did. As an adult, I finally learned that the Holy Spirit dwells inside every Christian and serves as an ever-present guide.

I love the parallels between a spotter and the Holy Spirit. Both of them are:

* True friends. The spotter isn't a stranger: he knows the driver well and may even be a family member. The Holy Spirit knows you intimately, too.

* Trustworthy. A driver trusts his spotter to make split-second decisions that affect the outcome of the race. We can trust the Holy Spirit, too, even when things in life are happening really fast or seem out of control.

* Good communicators. Spotters give specific direction to the driver when there's a problem, such as "Car in the wall in turn 4, stay low." When things are going well, the direction is still precise, such as, "You're clear of the 17 car." The Holy Spirit gives clear direction, too, whether life is going smoothly or whether you are experiencing difficulties.

Just like a driver listens closely to the spotter's directions, you can tune in to the Holy Spirit. He doesn't usually speak in an audible voice like a spotter on the radio. But when your heart is open to His leading, He guides you through scripture, circumstances or a peaceful confidence about what to do in a situation. While a human spotter might make a mistake sometimes, the Holy Spirit always gives perfect counsel. Are you tuned in?

Prayer: Dear God, thank you for providing a constant companion and guide in the Holy Spirit. Help me to be open to His leading as I go about my day. In Jesus' name, Amen.

Pit Stop

Have you ever been so upset that you could not think of what to pray? The Bible says that when we cannot find the words, the Holy Spirit intercedes for us and prays for us. Isn't that a comfort?

Most of the time we can pray just fine on our own, but we need to stay tuned in to our "Heavenly Spotter," the Holy Spirit. You can be bold when you pray. It's okay to pray, "Lord, please show me what to do. Please hit me over the head with it to make it very clear." Whether your race is going smoothly or whether you're heading into gray smoke, listen closely and trust the Holy Spirit to help, teach and guide you.

It's hard to hear Him speak to our hearts when there is too much external noise. Try this: When you pray, clear the airwaves by turning off the radio, music, phone and television. Can you hear Him now?

#3
Unexpected Blessings

Praise the Lord, O my soul, and forget not all his benefits.
Psalm 103:2

Has God ever surprised you with an unexpected blessing? My husband's friend, Frank, received a race day bonus that would thrill any race fan. A few weeks before the race, Frank told me about a ticket package he was considering and wanted to know if the price sounded reasonable. For each person, the package provided a bus ride to the track, a grandstand ticket and food. Upon hearing the price I said, "That's a great deal!"

But a great deal was about to become extraordinary. Frank and his two young sons boarded the bus and headed toward Dover International Speedway. Each bus passenger filled out a form which was used as an entry in a drawing. Frank's son won the prize and they received free tickets to sit in the Monster Bridge® – luxury seats right over the race track! They relaxed in air-conditioned comfort with head sets and monitors to see and hear the drivers on their in-car cameras. They enjoyed complimentary food and drinks and courteous V.I.P. treatment. Plus an unbelievable view of the cars racing straight toward them and zooming past under their feet.

Frank and his boys had a unique, clear view of the race through the Monster Bridge® windows. Sitting in comfort with the excitement and extravagance surrounding them, it was easy to be thankful for the privilege they received. Because the bridge contains only 56 seats which are not for sale, only a select few fans ever experience a race from its exclusive vantage point. Each and every moment, their circumstances were a constant reminder of the special blessing God provided.

It is easy to rejoice over unforeseen or lavish blessings which make us mindful of God's generosity. A new baby in the family. A gorgeous day for an outdoor wedding. An unexpected check in the mail. But are we any less blessed on ordinary days? It's easy to forget that we possess plenty of small and medium blessings all the time.

Sometimes we completely disregard the good things in life and focus on the negatives, especially when we're busy with our daily responsibilities. It's like when a driver is in traffic at 180 miles per hour, he only tells the crew chief when there's something wrong with the car. He might say, "I have a vibration" or "I'm wicked loose in the turns."

During a race you rarely hear statements like "Yep, the tires are spinning smoothly" or "Man, I'm grateful for my rearview mirror today." But later, when a driver isn't under the pressure of racing, he can take time to count his blessings and recall the positive aspects of the day.

Perhaps the trick to recognizing our blessings is to slow down and purposefully look for them. God is good all the time, not just when He sends big-time favor upon us. Take some time each day to praise Him for his abundant blessings – big ones, teeny tiny ones and even future benefits He has in store for you.

Prayer: Dear God, thank you for the bountiful blessings in my life. You are so good to me and I am ever grateful. In Jesus' name, Amen.

Pit Stop

Grab a notebook, a pen and your Bible. Read Psalm 103. In this chapter, David describes ways God showers us with love. This psalm promotes a grateful, heart-lifting frame of mind. Then make a list of the blessings in your life, from the petite ones to the enormous ones. When creating your list, keep in mind that blessings are not all material things. People, opportunities and situations can all be gifts from God.

Now think back to a time when God surprised you with a blessing. Build someone's faith by telling them about it.

#4
Drink Up!

Then God opened up the hollow place in Lehi, and water came out of it.
When Samson drank, his strength returned and he revived.
Judges 15:19a

Have you ever sat in the stands during a summer race and thought you would melt from the heat? It can get downright sweltering with the sun beating down on your head and only the scant brim of your driver cap to shade your face. Seasoned race fans know to pack a cooler or two full of cold drinks. For my family of four, I pack at least twenty bottles of water, iced tea and sports drinks for race day. Even so, we have sometimes resorted to buying extra drinks at the ridiculous price of three or four dollars each just to keep hydrated. Thirst is a powerful force!

Heat is an issue for drivers, too. Even on cool days, the heat from the engine makes in-car temperatures unbearable. In summer, the temperature inside the car can rise above 120 degrees. Whereas you can wear shorts and a t-shirt in the stands, the driver dons a fire suit, gloves, shoes and helmet. Phew! How can he keep cool?

Thankfully, the stock car has a cooling system that pumps cool air into the driver's helmet and up through holes in the seat. Fresh air enters through ducts in the right rear window and goes through a hose that blows directly over the driver at about elbow level. Since the floor of the car gets really hot, drivers wear special shoes with covers on their heels and soles.

Sometimes they add additional heat shields to avoid getting burned heels.

The extreme temperatures inside the race car are one reason race car drivers must be in top physical condition. Cardiovascular fitness is critical for enduring the heat and so is being properly hydrated. A driver can't down a few glasses of water on Sunday morning and be ready to roll. He has to start his hydration program midweek and drink enough liquid each day leading up to the race.

A driver can lose up to five to ten pounds of fluid during a single race simply from sweating and breathing out. If he doesn't replace the fluid, he becomes dehydrated and his performance suffers. He may develop a headache, mental fatigue, slower hand-eye coordination and decreased reaction times. That's why it is critical for a driver to drink during and after the race, too, to replace losses.

How much have you had to drink today? Keeping hydrated is as much a part of taking care of yourself as eating well and getting enough sleep. But in the busyness of each day, it is easy to forget to take in enough fluid. Feeling your best and performing well is as important for you as it is for your favorite NASCAR driver. If you find yourself with a slight headache or feeling sluggish in the afternoon, you may be dehydrated. Grab a glass of water or decaffeinated tea and revive with God's gift of refreshing liquids.

Prayer: Dear God, thank you for providing water and other beverages for me to hydrate my body and quench my thirst. Help me to care for my body by drinking enough each day. In Jesus name, Amen.

Pit Stop

Even Samson, the Bible strong man, could be brought to his knees by dehydration. After killing a thousand enemies with the jawbone of an ox, Samson was exhausted and extremely thirsty. He cried out to the Lord, "You have given your servant this great victory. Must I now die of thirst?" (Judges 15:18) God provided a spring for Samson to drink from, which refreshed and revived him.

If you have trouble remembering to drink enough, try a few of my strategies. First, drink a glass of water first thing when you get up, before eating or showering. It will be absorbed quickly and get your body processes off to a good start. Second, whether you're at work, at home or in the car, keep a bottle of fresh, cold water close at hand. Maybe throw in a slice of lemon or lime for flavor. Third, if water isn't your favorite, reward yourself with a glass of iced tea or other flavored beverage for every two glasses of water you drink. It may sound silly, but it works for me. Keeping yourself well-hydrated can make a difference in how you feel – drink up!

#5
A Heart Full of Joy

Restore to me the joy of your salvation and grant me a willing spirit, to sustain me.
Psalm 51:12

When Mark Martin wins a race, his infectious joy always makes me smile After winning the first race of the Chase in 2009, he joked around as if he thought he was dreaming. Mark climbed of his car in Victory Lane, grinned and said, "I'm sure I'm sleeping. Pinch me!"

Because of his joy, Martin can also lose graciously. He finished second in the 2007 Daytona 500, only two hundredths (0.020) of a second behind Kevin Harvick. Mark had never won a Daytona 500 and was understandably bummed out. In a post-race interview, he recapped the last moments of the race, then expressed gratitude to his US Army team and various individuals. In the face of an extremely disappointing loss, he offered thanks to those who helped him.

Sometimes the words joy and happiness are used interchangeably, but they are not the same. Happiness is a feeling that is based on our circumstances. But if things take a turn for the worse, we can suddenly become unhappy. Conversely, joy comes from within us. It is not determined by events of the day.

Joy begins when we realize the blessings we have as children of God. One blessing is that God loves us. Another is that we have the honor of being able to speak with almighty God at any time of the day or night – it's called praying. Plus we have the promise of heaven when we die. When we marvel at those privileges and allow gratitude to fill us, joy naturally wells up in our hearts. Then it spills over into our speech, attitudes and behaviors.

Just as parents love to see their children's delight as they open gifts on Christmas morning, God loves to see our joy in the blessings He has lavished upon us. Mark Martin seems to radiate that kind of Christmas joy through his words and demeanor.

On his 1000th career start in August 2009, Martin earned the pole at Bristol and came close to winning the race. After finishing second to Kyle Busch, Mark didn't act grumpy or complain. Instead, he chose to rejoice, telling a reporter, "For me - I've already had Christmas every day." Week in and week out, Mark Martin displays gladness whether he finishes first or fortieth, simply because he loves racing and chooses to focus on his blessings.

How about you – is your heart full of joy? If a reporter interviewed you as you climbed from your car after a frustrating day, what would you say?

Prayer: Dear God, I want to be joyful. Please help me to keep my focus on You and to be grateful for my blessings. In Jesus name, Amen.

Pit Stop

Joy is a beautiful thing, isn't it? When the Bible talks about "the joy of our salvation" it means the gladness we have in knowing our sins are forgiven and we're heaven-bound.

If you are not yet a child of God, you can be! You can pray right now to accept Jesus into your heart, no matter where you are.

Pray something like this: Dear God, I know I've done a lot of things wrong, but I want to be forgiven. I acknowledge that Your Son Jesus died to take the punishment for my sins and I want Him to be my Lord and Savior. I want to know the joy of salvation. Please come into my heart and accept me as your child. In Jesus' name, Amen.

You did it! This is the most significant decision of your life, so it's important to tell someone. If you know a pastor or another Christian, tell him or her that you prayed this prayer. Find a Bible-believing church where you can go to worship, make friends and learn more about God. Welcome to the family!

#6
Get Back on Track

*...let us throw off everything that hinders and the sin that so
easily entangles,
and let us run with perseverance the race marked out for us.
Hebrews 12:1b*

Drivers and crews will tell you that little things can mess
up a race. One place it can happen is on pit road. One tiny
misstep during a pit stop can throw off the whole crew's
rhythm and ruin the stop, causing the driver to lose track
position.

Let's say the driver overshoots the pit box and has to be
pushed back. The right rear tire changer will be thrown off by
having to pause before doing his job. It is even worse if he
already has the lug nuts off before the official asks the crew to
move the car. There are other things that can happen, like a
tire rolling out of the pit box or the car falling off the jack.
Seemingly small mistakes like these can be a big hindrance to
success.

Another mistake that can be costly is speeding on pit road.
For safety of crews and officials, pit road speeds are between
35 to 55 miles per hour, depending on the track. Punishment
for speeding might be a pass-through penalty or starting at the
tail of the longest line, which can cost the driver track position
or even put him a lap down. The driver might be staying below
the number on his tachometer that he thinks is the correct
speed. But if the calculations of the team engineers were off by
a teeny, tiny bit, the tachometer number can be wrong, causing

the driver to unintentionally speed on pit road, and get slapped with a penalty.

Mistakes happen during races. But it's important to get over them quickly. Wallowing in self-pity or self-anger is not appropriate or helpful. Everyone – the driver, crew chief and crew – must "untangle" themselves from whatever error was made and get their thinking back on track. The team analyzes what happened and takes steps to prevent another similar problem. The crew chief serves as an encourager, giving the crew a pep talk. Then each team member must persevere, bounce back from the mistake and do his best at the next pit stop.

Just like little mistakes can cause big problems during a race, little sins in our lives can have big consequences. Having lunch alone with a male coworker doesn't seem like such a big deal, until you start toying with the possibility of taking it further. Not claiming income on your tax forms for clients who pay cash seems harmless, until you are audited and fined. Even if you seem to get away with wrongdoing, God knows about it and so do you.

Everyone messes up. The trick is acknowledging the mistake and getting back on track. Throw off whatever is tempting you today. Get your thinking back to what is right and true and God-honoring. Be your own crew chief – look in the mirror and give yourself a pep talk. Encourage yourself to persevere in the race God has marked out for you.

Prayer: Dear God, when I mess up, please help me to get my thoughts and actions back on track. Thank you for forgiving me when I sin and helping me do better. In Jesus' name, Amen.

Pit Stop

Can you imagine how bad the tire changer feels when he forgets a lug nut and his driver has to come back to pit road? It must be tempting to have a pity party, but there's no time for that! He has to bounce back and do his best at the next pit stop.

The next time you mess up, don't wallow in it. Ask God to forgive you, then use it as an opportunity to learn. Do what the crew chief does: analyze what happened and learn from it. Throw off whatever bad thinking got you in trouble. Write down three specific changes to make - in what you think, say or do - to avoid repeating the same mistake. Those three strategies are your tools for getting back on track.

Bounce back from that sin and move forward. With God's help, you can do it!

#7
The Strongest Link

*The Lord is my strength and my shield; my heart trusts in
him, and I am helped.*
Psalm 28:7a

Dependability. Reliability. Two essential characteristics
for personnel on a race team. A race car driver depends on a
lot of people. He depends on his crew chief to make wise
decisions about adjustments and pit strategy. He relies on the
spotter to be his extra set of eyes on the track. He counts on his
pit crew to make fast, accurate stops. All week long, he needs
the guys in the shop to work hard to give him a top-notch car.

If one person makes a wrong decision, it can cost a driver
positions and points. Each link in the driver's "team chain"
must be dependable in order to achieve success.

To be dependable, a link must do what it is supposed to
do, day in and day out. As women, we serve as links in several
chains – our families, jobs and perhaps church, school or other
organizations. We do our best to be predictable and trustworthy
because lots of people count on us.

But sometimes stuff happens and we become a weak link
for a time. We arrive late to pick up the kids from soccer
practice. We mess up at work. We forget to wash our
daughter's gym uniform. We get sick. We're human, and
therefore fallible.

Links in a racing team can fail, too. Pit stops take too long.
A lug nut is too loose. Tires blow and engines fail. Stuff
happens both on the race track and in real life that is a direct

result of our undependable human nature.

There is only one totally dependable, completely reliable, 100 percent trustworthy person, and that's God. Everything else – people, machines, circumstances – will sometimes let us down. But God is constant - the strongest link.

No matter what is going on in your life, you can trust God. He is always there, faithful and steadfast in every situation. Is someone you love hurting? God listens when you pray for comfort and peace. Trouble with your teenager? God has the wisdom to show you what to do. He is your best friend who cares about every little detail, right down to lipstick and laundry and lug nuts.

Sometimes people think that when you become a Christian, life becomes a smooth ride with no problems, sadness or strife. That's simply not true. As long as we're living on earth, troubles are part of the human condition. The good news is that even when things go wrong or you face hardships, God is right there in the midst of it with you. He is waiting to offer strength, wisdom and comfort through prayer and the scriptures.

Is there something happening in your life that you haven't shared with God? Maybe you could do that today. Even if others have let you down, you can depend on Him. He is alive and real, ready to wrap you in his steadfast, loving arms. Faithful, reliable, dependable – that's who God is.

Prayer: Dear God, thank you for being the strongest link in my life. Help me to remember that when things go wrong and I'm overwhelmed, you are there for me, faithful and steady. In Jesus' name, Amen.

Pit Stop

God created the sun to be dependable. For as long as God allows this world to last, we can count on the sun hanging out in space, appearing to rise and set each day. Even when clouds block it from view, the great ball of fire is there, continuing to warm the earth from behind the scenes.

Do you like sunlight? I sure do! I love to close my eyes, tilt my face heavenward and savor the warmth. I feel like a sponge, soaking in strength and energy. God meant for people to enjoy the sunshine. When the sun's rays permeate our skin, our bodies synthesize vitamin D, which helps keep us healthy.

Doctors say most people are vitamin D deficient from spending so much time indoors. On average, people need about 15 minutes a day in the sun to make enough vitamin D. Do something good for your health - if weather permits, spend 15 minutes outside in the sunshine today. Let the sun's healing warmth wrap around you like the security of God's arms. When you see how good the sun makes you feel, you might get hooked and want to enjoy 15 minutes EVERY day!

#8
What's in a Name?

I will praise you forever for what you have done;
in your name I will hope, for your name is good.
Psalm 52:9

Some people are gifted with unique nicknames early in life. When my parents brought my baby sister home from the hospital, I was four years old. I looked at her tiny pink face and said, "Isn't she a little hon-o?" I must have been trying to say "honey," but it was too late. Our grandmother heard the nickname and made it stick. Despite her pretty name of Sondra, my sister is always called Hono by family and close friends.

Another way people get nicknames is from personality traits, talents or accomplishments. Richard Petty is called "The King" because he has more championships than any other driver in history. Ryan Newman was dubbed "Rocketman" when he set a qualifying record at Bristol during his sophomore racing year. That speedy name still fits because he has 45 poles to his credit as of this writing. Other drivers earned nicknames based on their driving styles, such as "The Intimidator" and "Smoke" – Dale Earnhardt, Sr. and Tony Stewart, respectively. Over the years, tracks have earned nicknames, too - Thunder Valley, the Monster Mile® and the Lady in Black, also known as Bristol Motor Speedway, Dover International Speedway and Darlington Raceway.

Another person who goes by more than one name is Jesus. His name comes from the Hebrew name, Yeshua, which means "salvation." But the Bible lists more than one hundred different names for Jesus, and each describes one of His attributes. Perhaps we could consider these His "nicknames" since they are derived from His multi-faceted character.

Some of my favorite biblical names for Jesus are the Good Shepherd, the Lamb of God, Wonderful Counselor, Prince of Peace, King of Kings, Savior and simply "Lord." No matter which title we call Jesus, His name is above every other name in history.

Sometimes people do not respect and value Jesus' name. Hearing the Lord's name abused by actors in movies or by people I know makes me shudder. People think that saying "Oh my God!" is no big deal. But unless you're praying or calling out to God for help, saying that phrase is taking the Lord's name in vain. Having a healthy fear of God helps a person refrain from mistreating Jesus' name. The Bible clearly states: You shall not misuse the name of the Lord your God, for the Lord will not hold anyone guiltless who misuses his name. (Exodus 20:7)

In this day and age, the names of God and Jesus are often shunned in the public square. But some boldly proclaim his name, like Morgan Shepherd with his "Victory in Jesus" car. Jesus wants us to talk about him and to pray in His name. I'm grateful that His name is made known at races through prayer. I love hearing the clergy close the invocation with Jesus' name during opening ceremonies. Makes me want to stand up and cheer before the race even begins. Go Jesus!

Prayer: Dear God, your name is precious to me. Guide my steps so that I many honor and glorify your name in all I do. In Jesus' name, Amen.

Pit Stop

Do you know what your first name means? Just for fun, look it up. Try an internet search using the phrase "What is the meaning of the name _____?" Don't be surprised if you find multiple meanings from different languages. For instance, my name, Beth, means "house of God" in Hebrew and "consecrated to God" in Old English.

Jesus has more meanings in His name than anyone who ever lived. That blesses us because the many names of Jesus can bring comfort for any situation. The next time you feel lost, think of Him as the Good Shepherd, finding His lost sheep and holding you close. If you feel alone, think of His name, Immanuel, which means "God with us." When you are stressed or afraid, try softly whispering the name of Jesus. The power of His holy name can melt away anxiety and bring you reassurance and peace.

#9

Wear Your Armor

Be strong in the Lord and in his mighty power. Put on the full armor of God
so that you can take your stand against the devil's schemes.
Ephesians 6:10-11

Stock car drivers know that what they do for a living is dangerous. It's not a matter of *if* they will crash, but when and how often. Drivers survive crashes due to their "armor" – the safety equipment on their bodies and in their cars. No driver would get into his car to compete without every single piece of his armor in place.

We are in a race, too, a battle for our very lives out in the world. Instead of skirmishing with other race cars, our combat is spiritual in nature. Although some people don't believe it, our adversary is real. We need to suit up every day in the armor of God.

It's interesting how closely the armor of God described in Ephesians 6 resembles the driver's armor:

Armor of God	**Driver armor**
belt of truth	seat belts and HANS device
breastplate of righteousness	firesuit
shoes of peace	fireproof shoes
shield of faith	face shield
helmet of salvation	helmet
sword of the spirit (Bible)	NASCAR rules

Let's look at the pieces of armor one by one:

Belt of truth: Truth is what we know about God and it is what holds everything in place, like a belt. In biblical times, soldiers wore thick belts that held their clothing together so they could fight. Likewise, the seat belts and HANS (Head And Neck Support) device hold the driver securely so he can drive.

Breastplate of righteousness: If you have accepted Jesus as your Savior, you are covered and protected by his righteousness. Likewise, the firesuit covers the driver to protect his skin and body from fire.

Shoes of peace: A soldier's shoes are his foundation, allowing him to stand firm and be ready to fight. We stand firm on the gospel of Jesus. Likewise, fireproof shoes allow the driver to keep his feet steady on the pedals. Without the shoes he would jiggle his feet to and fro, trying to avoid the heat on his heels.

Shield of faith: A shield protected a soldier from being injured by the enemies' weapons, such as arrows or swords. In a spiritual sense, standing behind your faith in God allows you to deflect the evil one's arrows of deception that he uses to confuse and weaken you. Likewise, a driver's face shield protects from flying debris or dust that might injure him or affect his eyesight.

Helmet of salvation: The helmet guards the head or the mind. A helmet is solid protection, just like Jesus is rock-solid as our salvation. Likewise, the driver's helmet is often his physical salvation, protecting his brain from life-threatening injury.

Sword of the spirit: The sword symbolizes the Bible,

which is a spiritual weapon. When we speak scripture out loud, it provides clarity and helps drive away confusion. Likewise, NASCAR has the power to create rules and clear guidelines that help teams and drivers make good decisions.

Speeding across a hard surface at 180 miles per hour only inches away from other cars is serious stuff. The only way a driver can feel secure enough to concentrate on his race is if all his safety equipment is in place. To use the full power of his talent and car, a driver must be wearing all of his protective gear.

You are running a tough spiritual race of your own. To give your best effort, you need to strap on your protective armor, too. Are you properly suited up for the race?

Prayer: Dear God, I want to wear the full armor so I can be effective for you in the race of my life. Help me to double check each day to make sure I have all my pieces of armor in place. In Jesus' name, Amen.

Pit Stop

Putting on God's armor is easier than you think. If you are a Christian*, you already have on three pieces of armor: your helmet of salvation, your breastplate of righteousness and your shoes of the gospel of peace.

Donning the rest of the armor takes some action on your part. What do you need to do? First, pick up your sword of the spirit and shield of faith by reading your Bible. Soaking up God's word will build your faith. Second, believe it! When you believe God's word is true, it is like tying on the last piece - your belt of truth, which holds the rest of your armor together. Now you're fully dressed and ready to face the day.

* If you would like to become a Christian, turn to the devotion called "A Heart Full of Joy" and read the Pit Stop for instructions.

#10
Family, Freedom and Faith

But as for me and my household, we will serve the Lord.
Joshua 24:15

You can feel the anticipation in the air when opening ceremonies begin at a race. First, the announcer reminds fans to remove their hats as our nation's flag is displayed. Next, a pastor prays for God's protection on the drivers, fans and crews. Then someone sings the National Anthem, with a military flyover during the closing lines.

While the anthem is sung, cameras pan from drivers and their wives and children to pit crews standing shoulder to shoulder. There is a feeling of hushed expectancy and reverence as the racing community shows esteem for the basic institutions of our nation: family, freedom and faith.

Races are family-friendly. Most tracks have family sections in the grandstands where no alcohol is allowed. Drivers' wives and children often accompany them trackside, spending time on pit road or in their motor homes. Some wives, like Kim Burton and Delana Harvick, often sit on the pit box during the race.

NASCAR honors the men and women of our armed forces by hosting military personnel as guests at many races. In addition, cars proudly display sponsors such as the Army, Navy, Air Force, Marine Corps, National Guard and Coast Guard.

Racing folks support our military off the track, too. For instance, drivers have visited injured soldiers at Walter Reed

Army Medical Center while en route to the Dover race. The Petty family has hosted bereaved military spouses and their children at Victory Junction camp.

Most exciting to me is that God has not been removed from these racing events. Just like Joshua took a bold stand that his household would serve God, racing folks have chosen to keep God in the sport. Many tracks have chaplains on staff. Other faith-based organizations, such as Motor Racing Outreach, organize events for fans on race weekends. Plus numerous drivers and their wives are Christians.

Honoring God, military and country was displayed during the Charlotte race weekend in May 2009. During pre-race ceremonies on Sunday, Amazing Grace was played by a trio of bagpipes. What a blessing to hear a hymn at a national sports event!

The race was rained out and held on Monday, which was Memorial Day. At 3:00 p.m., all 43 drivers stopped on the frontstretch, shut off their engines and joined Americans across the country in a moment of silence. Pit crews stood along the edge of the pit stalls in straight lines. In honor of those who served, silence blanketed the track and grandstands for a full minute. Tens of thousands of hearts focused on one hallowed purpose – remembering the men and women who serve our great country.

After the moment of silence, while everyone rustled back to their activities, commentator Darrell Waltrip put things in their proper perspective. He said, "This race is not nearly as important as the race we've got going on all over the world." He meant that what American troops deployed across the globe are doing is far more significant than a stock car race.

As race fans, we love our sport. But it is just that – a sport.

In the grand scheme of life, other things are far more important. Our families. The men and women who risk their lives for our freedom. Our faith in almighty God.

It is refreshing to watch a NASCAR race and see respect for those basic values. Makes you proud to be a fan, doesn't it?

Prayer: Dear God, I'm grateful that I can join in prayer with other fans before each race. Please bless our military families and protect our troops as they work to preserve our freedom. In Jesus' name, Amen.

Pit Stop

Have you ever wished you could do something to give back to our troops? You can! There are lots of ways to bless them through small acts of service such as writing cards of appreciation or sending items to brighten their days.

One organization I recommend is Operation Paperback (operationpaperback.org). You can box up a few new or gently used books and mail them to troops serving overseas. Go to their website and sign up, then indicate the genres of books you want to send. Operation Paperback provides an address of a serviceman or woman who has requested that type of books. Another organization that provides detailed information on how to supply a soldier with needed items from home is AnySoldier® (anysoldier.com).

Blessing the spouse and children of a deployed military person is a great way to show support, too. Lend a hand by providing a meal, babysitting or whatever else they need. Think of the comfort it brings to a soldier to know someone is helping his or her family at home. It's a great way to say "thank you!" to the dear souls who sacrifice for our freedom.

#11
Trouble on the Track

Is any one of you in trouble? He should pray.
James 5:13a

You're watching a race, enjoying the familiar rumble of engines as the cars speed by on your television screen. Suddenly one of the commentators cries, "There's trouble on the track!" Cameras switch to the action, whether it's a single car in the wall or a multi-car crash. Each driver in the field deals with the situation by doing something - heading down pit road, taking his car behind the wall or simply following the pace car around the track under the yellow.

Sometimes trouble appears quickly and without warning, like a bump from behind that sends a car spinning across the apron into the grass. Sometimes trouble brews between two drivers annoying each other throughout the race and culminates with one or both of them wrecked, black flagged or making a trip to the oval office to talk with race officials.

Real life can give us quick, unforeseen trouble, too. Sometimes the bumps are relatively small and easily resolved, like the new puppy peeing on the floor or the washing machine breaking down. Other times the bumps are the huge, take-your-breath-away kind such as your spouse losing his job or your teenage daughter telling you she is pregnant.

Sometimes trouble comes in the form of unpleasant relationships or situations that brew for a long time and then explode - like a conflict with a neighbor or a challenging relationship with a coworker or family member. Whether they are big or small, sudden or expected, how should we handle life's bumps?

When there's trouble on the track, a driver's instinct is to hold on tight, steer, brake or whatever else he needs to do to regain control. It is human nature to react physically and emotionally to a situation and try to manage it. But you know what? You better believe that a driver in trouble prays, too. And his wife sitting on the pit box? I believe her first reaction is to pray.

Sometimes we have difficult situations in life and we try to handle them on our own. We hold on tight, struggling and fretting and trying to regain control. We cry "I don't know what to do!" We try one tactic and it doesn't work out. We say the wrong thing and make the problem worse. We wish someone would guide us. Then we think, hmm, wait a minute... maybe I should pray. Uh, yeah!

Trying to fix the trouble yourself first and then praying is backwards. It's like trying to run a race without qualifying or practicing beforehand. Trying to deal with problems on our own is like a driver trying to discern a clear path through dense, gray smoke from a crash. We can't see the whole picture, but God can.

When trouble strikes on your track, pray first. Pray for wisdom. Pray for strength. Pray for patience. Listen for God's prompting of what to do and then do it. Through scripture and circumstances, He will steer you in the right direction and give you the right words.

Prayer: Dear God, forgive me for trying to handle problems on my own. Help me turn to You at the first sign of trouble, whether it's big or small. In Jesus' name, Amen.

Pit Stop

Think back to the last time you had a bump in your life. What did you do first? Have a good cry? Call your sister or a friend to pour out your heart and get her advice? E-mail your husband for help? Talking with friends, sisters and husbands can help us gain perspective and even some decent advice. Sometimes talking about the trouble stirs up our feelings even more and we end up even more stressed out.

On the other hand, telling God about your troubles can take away stress. Prayer is like a soothing balm that eases stress and gives you peace. God is the most trustworthy person in your life, and He is always, always, always the one to call first when you hit a bump in the road.

Give yourself a visual reminder to pray at the first sign of trouble. Treat yourself to a bracelet that has a cross or other Christian symbol on it. Wear it on the wrist you would use to reach for the phone so you see it and remember to call God first.

#12
Broken Scanner Blessings

Turn my heart toward your statutes and not toward selfish gain.
Turn my eyes away from worthless things; preserve my life according to your word.
Psalm 119:36-37

At the race track, I love wearing a scanner with head phones. That way I can listen to the announcers or the drivers' in-car radios. From time to time I take off the head phones and listen to the engines roar, especially on restarts. Love that sound!

One time my scanner died during a race. Even when I installed new batteries, it was silent. I was bummed out, but resigned myself to a race without chatter and just watched. I missed hearing the details of the race: who has a tire going down, what happened on pit stops, who is in line for the Lucky Dog and so on. Knowing the particulars gives the race depth and personality and makes the experience more fun for me.

To keep up with what was happening, I had two things to watch: the cars and the scoring pylon – a big pole with lighted numbers that show the running order. Since lapped cars were interspersed with lead lap cars on long green runs, the scoring pylon was the key to my understanding of the race. I learned something that day. Even though I relish listening to the commentators and the drivers, I really only need two basic things: the cars on the track and the pylon.

Without my scanner flooding me with information, I

focused on other things I might not have noticed, such as the people around me in the stands. I talked with my family more because I wasn't cocooned in my own little world of auditory stimulation. Despite the thunderous noise of the race, I felt a quietness in my spirit. I relaxed. I gazed around the track and soaked in the vivid colors, the smell of hot rubber and the rumbling engines. I focused on the vital race data - where my favorite driver was running and who was in the top ten. The simplicity was refreshing. In the end, the broken scanner was a blessing.

Then I thought about all the media I rely on – radio, television, internet, books, cell phone and so on. Am I allowing too much media and entertainment clutter to distract me from the really important things in life?

I began making comparisons about how I spend my time and energy. Which is more important - watching a television show or giving the kids my undivided attention? Reading another chapter in a book or listening to my husband talk about his day? Soaking in the latest political or sports news over breakfast or beginning my day with the Lord?

Time flies and kids grow up so fast. I don't want to regret the way I spent my time. In our media-laden culture, it's easy to get caught up in the endless flow of information and neglect the best parts of life – the people we love. Today, let's turn off some of the chatter and turn our hearts toward cultivating our relationship with God and our families.

Prayer: Dear God, I want to focus on the best things in life. Please guide me in knowing which distractions I need to filter out to make more time for You and the people I love. In Jesus' name, Amen.

Pit Stop

Do you ever feel overwhelmed by the car radio or the kids' video games or the television news? After a while it all becomes blah, blah, blah, yada, yada, yada. Trying to process myriad facts, flashing screens or constant music can be overwhelming. Too much sensory input can wear you down. Sometimes I just want to scream "Turn it all off!"

In addition to giving us more time for people in our lives, reducing media intake can refresh the soul and reduce stress. Silence is therapeutic. Sights and sounds of nature are soothing.

Look around your home at the ways media is being used. Is there anywhere you can make a change to limit the noise and increase family interaction? For example, remove the television from eating areas and declare mealtimes to be media-free. Or turn off music in the car sometimes and talk instead. Get a CD of soothing nature sounds to play once in a while. Find ways to turn the blah, blah, blah into aahhh.

#13
Big Faith, Big Heart

"I tell you the truth, if you have faith as small as a mustard seed,
you can say to this mountain, 'Move from here to there' and it will move.
Nothing will be impossible for you."
Matthew 17:20

When I think of racing-related charities, the first one that comes to mind is Victory Junction Camp in North Carolina. The camp gives children with chronic medical conditions and serious illnesses a once-in-a-lifetime experience full of laughter and love in a medically-supervised environment. Kyle Petty and his wife, Pattie, founded the camp in honor of their son, Adam, who was killed in a crash during a Nationwide practice session in 2000. Land for the camp was donated by Richard and Lynda Petty, Adam's grandparents.

Adam Petty liked to visit sick kids in the hospital and dreamed of building a special camp for them someday. When the teenager voiced his dream out loud, someone told him it would bankrupt the family business. Adam's response? He said he worked for a "big God" who could do anything! Today, Adam's dream is a reality and has blessed more than 12,000 children and their families at this writing.

Living with a serious illness or persistent medical issues is a big burden for a youngster. But Victory Junction provides a safe place to do fun, empowering activities that make kids feel larger-than-life. Imagine being the parent of a camper and seeing the joy on your child's face. For those parents and children, being part of the Victory Junction Gang must seem like heaven on earth.

Have you noticed that people who have big faith often have a big hearts, too? That's because people who love Jesus feel compelled to share His love with others. It's a wonderful, continuous circle where we love others, which expands our hearts, which grows our faith, so we love others more, grow a bigger heart, grow even more faith, and so on. A big faith leads to big dreams and selfless giving to others.

Victory Junction Camp started with one idea and faith that was way bigger than a mustard seed. Adam Petty's steadfast faith in God coupled with the loving dedication of his family led to his big-hearted dream being fulfilled. Today that dream has almost doubled because the Petty family is working on building a second camp in Kansas.

Is there something specific you dream of doing to help people? Do you have a talent you want to use in service to others? Perhaps you enjoy painting or landscaping or planning banquets and have an idea how you could use your abilities to benefit your neighbors, church or a charity. Maybe you want to adopt an orphan or get your bone marrow checked to see if you're a match for someone.

Whatever your desire, God planted the seed in your heart and you must take action to bring it to fruition. Step out in faith. God will help you and provide opportunities for you to work toward your dream.

Race Fans' Devotions to Go

Prayer: Dear God, I want to be a blessing to others by using my talents in service. Show me how to channel my dreams into action so that I can best serve others and build my faith in the process. In Jesus' name, Amen.

Pit Stop

Want to help a NASCAR-related charity? Visit the Victory Junction Camp website at www.VictoryJunction.org to learn about ways you can lend a hand. If you knit or sew, you can help the camp in a unique way by crafting afghans, pillows or quilts for campers. You can also make a financial contribution, donate items on their Wish List or apply to be a camp volunteer.

There are other ways you can join with the racing community to help others. Many, many drivers have foundations that help kids. For example, the Kasey Kahne Foundation raises funds for charities that care for chronically ill children and their families. The Denny Hamlin Foundation and the Jeff Gordon Foundation both help kids with cancer.

The Hendrick Marrow Program helps bone marrow transplant patients by paying for treatments and raising money to add more potential marrow donors to the registry. The Greg Biffle Foundation and the Ryan Newman Foundation work to improve the well-being of animals. These are just a few of the racing-related charities out there. Check your favorite driver's website or the NASCAR Foundation for ways you can help.

#14

Facing our Fears

So we say with confidence, "The Lord is my helper; I will not
be afraid.
What can man do to me?"
Hebrews 13:6

Have you ever taken a ride in a stock car? As of this writing, I have not had that privilege. The thought of zooming around a race track at high speeds both terrifies and exhilarates me. If I could climb into the car with a guarantee that we wouldn't crash into the wall, I would do it in a heartbeat. What holds me back? Fear.

Even with all the safety equipment, driving a stock car at 180-plus miles per hour is dangerous. Add in forty-two other competitors driving inches apart and you have a recipe for "the big one."

Each driver's wife has probably been afraid at one time or another during her husband's career. These courageous women have learned to overcome their fears and watch their husbands go racing week in and week out. How can we conquer our week in and week out worries?

The first order of business is to pinpoint what we're afraid of. There are good, normal fears that prompt us to behave in ways that keep us safe – like backing away from a snarling dog, locking our doors at night or waiting until the sign says "walk" to cross the street. These are healthy, God-given apprehensions that help us survive day-to-day without harm.

Unhealthy fears are the ones we need to scrutinize under

the magnifying glass of God's truth. These are the worries that cripple us emotionally and keep us from stepping out in faith. A fear of flying, crowds, rejection or strangers may limit what we can do if we allow the panic to take over. It is not wrong to fear any of these things. But what if your anxiety stops you from doing something the Lord has asked you to do?

If God has called you to teach Sunday school but you decline because you're afraid of public speaking, that is a shame. If you want to take a batch of cookies to your new neighbors, but are afraid you won't know what to say to them, your fear is keeping you from blessing others. God calls us to step out in faith despite the fear, even when we have shaky knees and butterflies in our stomachs.

Stepping out in faith requires courage. It means doing things, even hard and scary stuff, despite our qualms and doubts. But thankfully, we're not alone in facing our monsters.

Someone has said, "Courage is fear that has said its prayers." How true! Prayer can fortify us with supernatural strength to do what we need to do, despite our worries.

Are there fears in your life that you allow to control you? Ask God to fill you with courage and power to step out of your comfortable places into the exciting unknown. Walk through the fear, remembering that the God of the universe is carrying you each step on the path He has planned for you.

Prayer: Dear God, I don't want doubts and worries to hinder the plans You have for me. When I'm afraid, help me to focus on You alone. Give me power and authority to ignore the uncertainties and walk forward in faith. In Jesus' name, Amen.

Pit Stop

I love the high speed thrill of NASCAR - as a spectator, that is. How can I love speed and fear it at the same time?

I've heard it said that fear and faith cannot exist together, but I disagree. I believe we can have an emotional fear of doing something, yet through faith, receive the courage to actually do it. It's called facing our fears.

Think about your life. What hopes and dreams have you allowed to fade because of fear? Below is a list of verses about fear and faith. Look them up. Pray them. Step out in faith!

Isaiah 41:13
Psalm 9:10
Psalm 46:1
Proverbs 3:24-26
John 14:27
Romans 8:15
Ephesians 6:16
2 Corinthians 5:7
2 Timothy 1:7
Hebrews 13:6

#15
Know the Backstory

Lord, who may dwell in your sanctuary? He whose walk is blameless and who does what is righteous, who speaks the truth from his heart and has no slander on his tongue, who does his neighbor no wrong and casts no slur on his fellow man.
Psalm 15:1a, 2-3

Racing is more than cars zipping around in circles. Seasoned fans know there are background details or "backstory" that makes the sport fascinating. When they learn these nuances, rookie fans realize that what appears to be simple is often quite complicated.

Take qualifying, for instance. To an outside observer, it appears that drivers have a level playing field during qualifying. They each drive two laps on the same track. The running order is determined by a random lottery-like drawing of numbers. That's sounds fair and simple, right?

But it isn't. There is backstory, a critical fact about qualifying that isn't obvious: the surface temperature of the track affects speed – hotter is slower, cooler is faster. Since track temperature varies throughout the day due to air temperature and sunshine, some drivers might have an advantage over others.

A cooler track temperature gives the tires more grip which means a faster qualifying lap. So at tracks where the sun goes down during qualifying, drawing a spot near the end is an advantage. Sometimes the sun going behind the clouds for a few minutes cools the track enough to make a difference. If you watch qualifying without knowing how weather affects the track, you don't have the whole picture.

Another bit of racing backstory is that rain can change track conditions. When it rains before a race, jet dryers are used to blow the track dry. The huge whoosh of forced air pushes some of the marbles (rubber bits from the tires) off the track, cleaning it off and making it slick.

A wise crew chief knows not to over-adjust his car during the first pit stop of the race while the track is still on the slick side. Why? Because as the race goes on, the track rubbers up pretty quickly creating more traction and he wants his car to run well in those conditions.

Knowing the backstory helps a crew chief make appropriate decisions. He waits until he has all the relevant information before making judgment calls. That's a good example for us to follow, too.

Relationships and situations in life can be as unpredictable as race track conditions. Circumstances that appear simple on the surface might actually be complicated. If we make snap judgments or premature statements, we run the risk of misjudging someone or even slandering them – all because we don't know their backstory.

Have you ever met someone and thought, "Well, she's kind of snobbish." Or rude or bossy – you get the idea. That woman may have a difficult backstory in her life that causes her to act a certain way. For example, a coworker who seems unfriendly and distant may be emotionally drained from caring for her chronically ill child or an aging parent. Learning her backstory allows you to sympathize instead of criticize.

A wise woman holds her tongue when she's not sure of all

the facts. She keeps her thoughts and words unassuming and kind, giving people the benefit of the doubt. Because her heart is compassionate, she casts no slur on anyone and speaks only when she is sure of the truth.

Is there a complicated person, relationship or situation in your life? Make the effort to learn the backstory so you can respond in an honorable fashion.

Prayer: Dear God, I don't want to make rash judgments or speak harshly of others. Please give me discernment about what people are going through so I can respond in an informed and empathetic manner. In Jesus' name, Amen.

Pit Stop

In order to know someone's backstory, we need to spend time with them. Sometimes relationships suffer because in the busyness of life, we have lost touch with each other.

One way to reconnect is to have a mini-retreat. If your family or a girlfriend or two are willing, plan a get-together where you concentrate on bonding. It can be anything from a game night around the kitchen table to a whole weekend getaway at a hotel or cabin. Plan some fun activities, but leave plenty of time for just hanging out doing nothing, so you can talk to each other. You never know what backstory you might learn that will promote deeper understanding and bring you closer.

#16
Red Flag Moments

There is a time for everything, and a season for every
activity under heaven.
Ecclesiastes 3:1

Even people who don't follow racing have heard of the Daytona 500, the first points race of the NASCAR season. As a restrictor plate race, it is known for bumper to bumper action from start to finish. When "the big one" occurs, drivers and teams might get a bit of down time during a long caution or a red flag while the debris is removed and the track is swept clean.

During the 52nd running of the Daytona 500 in 2010, the drivers did more sitting still than usual. The race was red-flagged twice to repair the track in turns one and two where a chunk of the pavement came loose.

Safety crews patched the hole each time, allowing adequate time for the patching product to set. Meanwhile, the teams, drivers and fans had some down time on their hands. The drivers got out of their cars and stretched their legs. Even though they were not thrilled with the delay, they made the best of it by using the time wisely. They used the rest room and chatted with team members. Some refreshed themselves with a drink and snack, like Jimmie Johnson and Mark Martin, who munched on power bars. Kyle Busch closed his eyes for a brief catnap. Other drivers joked around on camera, such as Carl Edwards, who teased teammate David Ragan about swiping half of his sandwich. I suspect fans walked around the stands, visited the rest rooms and bought refreshments and souvenirs while they waited for the race to resume.

The reporters kept busy on pit road, filling up the empty airtime with driver interviews so the fans at home were entertained. The television announcers kept viewers informed with updates on track repairs and other interesting tidbits. All in all, the media and racing folks did a good job handling the unforeseen down time with poise and humor. Everyone got busy doing something that benefited themselves or someone else.

Have you ever been hit with unexpected down time? Maybe you broke your leg or had an extended recovery period after surgery. Maybe you lost your job and the days seemed to stretch out in front of you with no end in sight. Or perhaps you had to wait for an hour at the doctor's office or in traffic. What do you do with blocks of unfilled time?

When you find yourself temporarily red-flagged, view it as a gift instead of a waste of time. Take a moment to refuel and refresh with a drink or a snack. Make a list of people you know who are going through a tough time and pray for them. Write an encouraging note to a friend. Read a devotion or scripture. Create a menu of healthy suppers for the rest of the week and write your grocery list. Call a friend or relative you haven't talked with for a while. Do a crossword puzzle or Sudoku to stimulate your memory. The possibilities are endless! By the time your waiting is over, you will have nurtured yourself or someone else, leaving you feeling productive and joyful instead of irritated or bored.

The racing community made fruitful use of unexpected down time during extended red flags. Will you follow their example?

Prayer: Dear Lord, when I'm surprised with empty time on my hands, help me to use it to bless myself or others in some way. In Jesus' name, Amen.

Pit Stop

Keep a few things in your purse, car or nightstand to use during unexpected down times. Some ideas are bottled water, a few snacks, a puzzle book, a notebook and pen for journaling or making lists, a few blank note cards, a pocket-sized devotional book like this one or a small Bible. The next time you are red-flagged, relax! Waiting doesn't have to be drudgery. Enjoy the gift of free time to use in whatever fruitful way you choose.

#17
Loose In, Tight Off

Do not let any unwholesome talk come out of your mouths,
but only what is helpful for building others up according to
their needs, that it may benefit those who listen.
Ephesians 4:29

During a race, you may hear a driver say that his car is "loose in, tight off," referring to how the car is handling in the turns. It means the car is loose going into the turns and tight exiting the turns.

When a car is loose, the back tires lose traction and the rear end tries to fishtail, making the driver feel like he's going to spin out. Conversely, a tight race car feels like it doesn't want to turn because the front tires are losing traction while the rear tires push the car forward.

"Loose in, tight off" could also describe our lips when we say something we shouldn't (loose lips in) and then regret it (tight lips off.) When our lips are loose they can spew all kinds of unwholesome talk: gossip, complaints, criticism and angry barbs. At the very least, these words can leave us with a rearview mirror full of regret, wishing we could take them back.

Imagine a race commentator describing it: "There she goes through turn one with her loose lips flapping – yackitty yack yack. Lips still loose through turn two and all the way across the back stretch. But wait, going into turns three and four her lips are sealed tight. Yessiree, tight lips through the front stretch. She's quiet on the radio, ladies and gentlemen, wishing she hadn't said those things. Now she's heading down pit road for some adjustments to make sure that loose lips problem doesn't happen again."

At worst, unwholesome words can spin out of control, ending in a big wreck that injures others and damages our own character. It would be great if the splattered mess of ugly words could be removed as simply as a windshield tear-off, wouldn't it? But sadly, the dents caused by angry words cannot be repaired as easily as bent sheet metal.

Loose lips and loose cars both cause wrecks. Fortunately for drivers, when a race car is loose, the pit crew can make adjustments, such as taking air out of the right rear tire or lowering the track bar. These small changes should make the car handle better in the corners and give the driver more control.

Are there adjustments we can make to prevent loose lips, too? I think so. For me, loose lips occur most often when I am hasty. When I judge a situation too quickly or give in to speedy irritation, my negative thoughts become frustrated words. Being fast is an advantage on the race track but speed is often a drawback for translating thoughts into spoken words.

When negative emotions hit, I need to throw the caution flag, decelerate and pause before speaking. Instead of taking air out of a tire, the slowdown takes air out of my *ire*. Funny, huh? That brief recess gives me more control and I'm less likely to display loose lips.

When I step back for a moment, I tend to give others the benefit of the doubt. So many misunderstandings could be cleared up instead of blown up, if we would speak well of others instead of spouting complaints based on what we think we know.

Next time you feel negative words bubbling up, pull into your pit stall and pause for an adjustment. It's easier than trying to clean up the debris resulting from loose lips.

Prayer: Dear God, I don't want to say words that wreck feelings and hurt relationships. Help me to avoid the unwholesome talk of loose lips and say caring, helpful things instead. In Jesus' name, Amen.

Pit Stop

Just like proper balance helps prevent a loose race car, the right perspective helps us steer clear of loose lips, too. For me, a good pre-race adjustment is putting in a "half round" of scripture. Or taking pressure out of my annoyance by praying. Doing these things keeps me in a better frame of mind so I remember to pause before speaking.

For the next week, make a conscious effort to pause every time something or someone irritates you. Try to put a positive spin on the situation by giving the person the benefit of the doubt. Maybe your coworker has a family problem on her mind. Maybe the store clerk is stressed because her car broke down and made her late for work. Maybe your child's coach is exhausted or has a headache, or both! Having empathy may help you to say something friendly or kind.

Pause. Give people the benefit of the doubt. Don't give loose lips a chance to wreck your day.

#18
Listening to the Crew Chief

The LORD came and stood there, calling as at the other
times, "Samuel! Samuel!"
Then Samuel said, "Speak, for your servant is listening."
I Samuel 3:10

Have you ever watched a race where one of the drivers has lost radio communication with his crew chief? That must be a terrible feeling for both of them. The driver is racing round and round, unable to give the crew chief any information about the car. He has no idea when he is supposed to pit or whether it will be a two-tire or four-tire stop. He can't even hear the crew chief count him into the pit stall. That poor driver is on edge, feeling restless and disconnected from the rest of his team.

Although the driver holds the steering wheel and controls the car, the crew chief is the team leader. He provides wise advice and direction from atop the pit box. Without his crew chief's guidance, a driver can make independent decisions, but they may not be the best ones. Crew chiefs are equipped to see the big picture and may be privy to information the driver doesn't have.

Drivers and crew chiefs spend a great deal of time together during the week. They discuss every little detail about the car, their team and their plans for both. They converse a lot. When one talks the other listens, and vice versa.

What would happen if the driver talked constantly and never let his crew chief talk? Or what if when the crew chief talked, the driver was distracted and didn't really listen. Do you think that driver would be equipped to meet the challenges of the next race? Nope. A wise driver listens closely to his crew chief.

In real life, you are like the race car driver and God is like your crew chief. Listening to His direction is essential for you to be prepared to meet life's challenges. But it's up to you to keep the lines of communication open.

Have you ever felt restless in your spirit, like a driver without radio contact? Do you ever feel an anxious anticipation, like you're waiting for something, but you don't know what? That edgy, frustrated feeling may mean you are disconnected from your crew chief. It may mean God is trying to speak to you.

In the Bible, the boy Samuel was trying to sleep, but kept hearing someone call his name. After it happened several times, Eli the priest told Samuel it was God trying to get his attention. So the next time he heard the Lord's voice, Samuel said, "Speak, for your servant is listening."

When God calls your name through an expectant feeling in your spirit, let Him know you are listening. Take steps to open the line of communication by praying and then listening for His voice. Don't keep racing without the wisdom and direction of your crew chief. Follow Samuel's example and let God know you are ready to hear from Him.

Prayer: Dear God, thank you for being willing to speak to me, even though I sometimes forget to listen. Help me to always be ready to hear your voice calling my name. In Jesus' name, Amen.

Pit Stop

Do you want to hear from God? Me, too! There is nothing in this world like the feeling of knowing that God has spoken directly to your heart.

Remember the example of drivers and crew chiefs. They spend time together and take turns talking and listening. A good way to hear from God is to spend a lot of time with Him during the week. Each day, choose a passage of scripture – anywhere from a couple of verses to a chapter. Read it and meditate on it. Read it over and over if you need to. Think about what the verses mean. Sit quietly and expectantly, asking God to show you what He wants you to learn or apply to your life.

Talk to God in prayer, too, sharing your praises and concerns. Ask any questions you have about the scripture and continue to listen for His answers. If you have trouble being quiet without your mind wandering, you're not alone. When you find your thoughts drifting, just bring them back to God and keep listening, even as you go about your day.

#19
People-to-People Stuff

*I the Lord search the heart and examine the mind
to reward a man according to his conduct...*
Jeremiah 17:10

My husband and sons aren't particularly interested in watching pre-race coverage. They usually tune in during opening ceremonies just in time to hear the command. On the other hand, I look forward to pre-race reporting - driver interviews, bits of trivia and good-natured banter among the commentators. I love hearing what the drivers did during the week – who held a charity event or who went fishing together. Hearing snippets of news about crew members and details about drivers and their families is fascinating to me.

After a race, my family was walking down an access road toward the parking lot when we heard a gentle "beep-beep" behind us. Realizing a car wanted to get through the pedestrians, I turned to see how close it was. I looked through the windshield of an SUV, an arm's length away. Behind the wheel was Ryan Newman with his wife, Krissie in the passenger seat. I was thrilled! I smiled at them and thought to myself, "Now I can tell people I was almost run over by a NASCAR driver!" Not true really, because Ryan was very cautious, driving s-l-o-w-l-y through the sea of race fans. But it made for a fine story to tell my friends.

Seeing Ryan and Krissie Newman from a few feet away was the icing on the race day cake for me. Why do I savor "people-to-people stuff" while my guys stick to the action?

Perhaps it's a girl thing. Although we love engines and three-wide racing as much as men do, women are captivated by relationships and emotion, even in a spectator sport. I want to hear Jeff Burton on the in-car audio praising his crew for a good pit stop. I want to see Kim Burton's expression when Jeff is leading with ten laps to go. When Kurt Busch wins a race, I need to see his reaction when the guy who spun him around on lap 84 approaches him in Victory Lane.

What are we looking for when we watch the interactions between drivers, crews, officials and others? Some fans like to see a drivers get testy with each other, on and off the track. Snide remarks, blame games or a little push-and-shove make for a good soap opera and fodder for tomorrow's newspaper stories and sports talk shows. But is that the kind of drama we crave from professional athletes?

How about cheering when a driver takes responsibility for a track mishap or apologizes for crowding another guy against the wall? That's humility. Maybe we should wave our hats when the winner credits his crew chief with making the pit road call that clinched the race. That's giving credit where it's due. I love hearing the second place driver in a photo finish give an upbeat post-race interview, congratulating the winner, thanking his crew and sponsors, even though he's disappointed about missing the win by inches. That kind of gracious "people-to-people stuff" we see so often from drivers makes me proud to be a NASCAR fan.

When your favorite driver shows good sportsmanship toward competitors and gratitude for his crew, it deserves as much celebration as a good finish. Let's root for success and character, on the track and in the people-to-people stuff, too.

Prayer: Dear Lord, help me to notice and acknowledge when others do the right thing. In Jesus' name, Amen.

Pit Stop

Actively look for opportunities to compliment others when they show character traits like humility or generosity. Make it a habit to point out three each day. For example, tell your husband you're proud of how he handled a situation with the neighbors. Praise your teenage daughter who volunteers as a math tutor for a younger child. Thank a friend for calling just to say hi. Notice the positive people-to-people stuff going on around you and celebrate it!

#20
The Lucky Dog

Grace and peace to you from God our Father and the Lord Jesus Christ.
1 Corinthians 1:3

My friend, Leslie, signs her e-mails with the closing of "Grace & Peace." I love that she puts grace first, because a person must receive God's grace first in order to have His peace.

Grace is one of those words whose meaning seems vague, but it is actually quite simple. What exactly is it? Grace means unmerited favor. It's a gift given to someone who doesn't deserve it.

Peace is the deep-down knowledge that you are saved. It is a feeling of relief and trust that no matter what happens, you are going to be okay because you are a child of God. Peace follows grace because after you receive grace through God's free gift of salvation, you feel peace.

When I think of grace, it reminds me of a rule in racing that gives unmerited favor to one driver. It's called the beneficiary rule, at least that's the official name. Most people just call it the Lucky Dog or the free pass.

When the caution flag flies, the first driver who is a lap behind gets the "Lucky Dog." That means he can drive around to the tail end of the line and become the last car on the lead lap. Instead of being a lap down, the Lucky Dog driver is now back on the lead lap, which puts him back in the running to win. Getting the Lucky Dog is so important that the first two lapped cars will battle for position just as hard as the leaders.

Anytime a driver gets the Lucky Dog, he feels happy, with a sense of relief about being back in the hunt. He has received an unearned gift, the grace of NASCAR, if you will. He didn't work his way back onto the lead lap by passing the leader under green. The lap was simply gifted back to him as a result of the Lucky Dog rule.

Getting back on the lead lap can have huge impact on a race, especially for a driver who has a fast car that handles well. It is not uncommon to see such a driver have a minor problem that puts him a lap down, then get the Lucky Dog and work his way to the front to win the race.

The next time you see a driver get the Lucky Dog, think of grace and peace. That driver got a free gift he didn't deserve – that's grace. Now he is relieved to be back on the lead lap - that's peace.

The best thing is that God sees us all as Lucky Dogs. He is eager to extend grace to each and every one of us. If we believe in Jesus, God gives us a free pass into heaven. He extends grace and we receive peace.

Prayer: Dear God, thank you for your gift of grace and the peace it brings to my life. In Jesus' name, Amen.

Pit Stop

Today's verse is the greeting of a letter the apostle Paul wrote to one of his churches. Whereas Paul used "grace & peace" as a greeting, my friend Leslie uses the phrase as a closing. Either way, the person on the receiving end is blessed.

Just like God extends grace to us, we can do the same for others. Is there someone in your life who irritates you often? Or someone at work who seems to always be a lap down by being behind in their work? Does one of your children dawdle frequently instead of getting chores or homework done? Think of something you could do to extend grace (unmerited favor) to that person today.

Here are some ideas to get you started, but feel free to be creative and come up with your own, too:

*Say something kind or complimentary to someone who usually irritates you.

*Buy a "lapped" coworker a cup of gourmet coffee on the way to work and leave it on her desk with an encouraging sticky note. Use "grace & peace" with your signature.

*On a night when your child has extra homework, give him a special snack (before dinner!) while he's working on it.

Grace & peace to you, my friend!

#21
Sticky Tires, Sticky Sin

Have mercy on me, O God, according to your unfailing love;
according to your great compassion blot out my
transgressions.
Wash away all my iniquity and cleanse me from my sin.
Psalm 51:1-2

When you step in dirt, wiping your feet on a mat or in the grass cleans off the bottom of your shoes. Tires on race cars get dirty, too. Race tracks are covered with tiny bits of rubber called marbles that stick to the tires during a race. There is a special way to clean off the tires by "wiping" them on the track.

As a driver follows the pace car, he turns the steering wheel back and forth repeatedly, swerving left and right as if he's going around cones in an obstacle course. This to-and-fro action rubs the off the rubber debris sticking to the tires. All the drivers do this tire-cleaning maneuver, keeping the swerving within a tight radius so they don't accidentally veer into each other.

Some things are harder to clean off than shoes or tires. Have you ever tried to clean sticker goo off a book? For some reason, stores tend to place price stickers on the front covers of new books. When you pull the sticker off, there is often a gunky residue left in its place. If you don't remove it, dust and dirt gets trapped in the goo and looks messy.

The things is, removing the goo is a pain and leaves a scar behind. Whether you scrape it off or use nail polish remover to dissolve it, the book cover is usually marred. So your choices are to leave the ugly sticker on the book, take it off and let the goo get gunkier or remove the goo and disfigure the book. Ugh - none of the choices allows an unspoiled, sticker-free book cover!

Sometimes I make a similar mess with my thoughts and words. Thinking something unkind is ugly. It's like a sticker with the yucky goo underneath, but at least it is hidden where it can't hurt anyone. But sometimes I let the thought form critical words that come out of my mouth and offend someone – like peeling off the sticker and exposing the gooey glue. Then I say something else to try and fix it, but those words get tangled in the goo and make it worse - gooier and stickier. I end up like the book cover, with my sinful words clinging to me in an unsightly way.

Does stuff ever stick to you? It's easy to get down on ourselves when we do wrong and feel grimy – like there's stuff sticking to us. Sin is very sticky. The way we clean it off is by repenting - asking God to forgive us and getting cleansed by the blood of Jesus. The great thing about being forgiven is that sin-removal doesn't leave us marred, like the book cover. We end up clean and shiny with no sticky residue of sin anywhere in sight – cleaner than a set of brand new tires!

Confessing sin to God is just like talking to a friend. There's nothing fancy or lofty you need to say. Just tell Him what you did wrong. Ask Him to forgive you and help you avoid that sin in the future. Being forgiven means that sticky sin falls away, leaving you as clean as a white flag. Halleluiah!

Prayer: Dear God, I'm so grateful that you forgive me freely when I repent. Thank you for allowing Jesus' blood to pardon my sins and cleanse me from the sticky snare of sin. In Jesus' name, Amen.

Pit Stop

A funny thing happens in my home. Things get moved from where they belong and "stick" to other locations in the house. Does that happen where you live?

Getting rid of junk, clutter and dirt makes us feel refreshed and more relaxed. In fact, clutter can even contribute to stress. Yuck, who needs that?

To decrease stress and tidy things up, try this quick pick-me-up. Go through your house and put away ten things that are not in their places. Anytime you feel stressed, return a few sticky things to their places. It feels great!

#22
Supporting Your Sponsor

We are therefore Christ's ambassadors, as though God were making his appeal
through us. We implore you on Christ's behalf: Be reconciled to God.
2 Corinthians 5:20

The phrase "silly season" is a new expression for me, even though it's been around for years. It's slang for the last half of the racing season when rumors circulate about which drivers might change teams or sponsors. Silly season speculation seems to begin earlier and earlier each year, especially about drivers who are approaching the end of their contracts.

When a driver changes teams, he often gets a new sponsor. But sometimes things work out that the old sponsor sticks with the driver and goes along to the new team.

The relationship between a driver and his sponsors, especially the primary sponsor, is vital to a team's success. A primary sponsor pays big bucks to have the company name on the car hood and on the team uniforms, so drivers need to do certain things to honor the sponsor. A driver always represents his sponsor during his post-win interview in Victory Lane. He doesn't just say "My car was great today." He specifically mentions "the DuPont Chevrolet" or "the DeWalt Ford" and thanks other sponsors by name, too.

Even off the track, drivers are ambassadors for their sponsors. A driver makes appearances on behalf of the company who backs his car financially, signing autographs or doing question-and-answer sessions or other personal appearances. The associate sponsors, who have logo stickers on the car, receive a certain number of driver appearances each year as well. When a driver wins, he does the "hat dance" in Victory Lane, posing for a gazillion photos wearing different baseball caps with logos for every sponsor of his car.

When you watch television or shop for groceries, you see the names of companies that sponsor racing teams. Have you ever had the jingle from a commercial stuck in your head? Have you bought a food product because there's a photo of a driver on the package? That makes sponsors very happy!

Whether it is life insurance, home or office supplies or candy, fans link the drivers with the names of companies who sponsor them. Then dedicated NASCAR fans like us buy sponsor products and driver merchandise to show our loyalty.

This whole sponsorship and fan loyalty thing got me thinking: Do I show more outward devotion to my favorite driver than to God? On race day, people can take one look at my outfit and know which driver I support. But can they tell I belong to Jesus?

Most of us don't go around with "Jesus" embroidered on our caps or painted on our cars. But we are still His ambassadors. We represent Him, just like a driver represents his sponsor, through everything we do and say. And the best thing is there's no silly season with God where you have to worry about losing Him as your sponsor. Once you accept Him, He supports you for life.

Prayer: Dear God, as your ambassador to the world, I want to bring you honor. Help me to point others to You every day through my actions and words. In Jesus' name, Amen.

Pit Stop

A rookie driver is required to do many personal appearances so that fans get to know his face and associate his name with his sponsor's product. By acting as an ambassador, the driver helps build a following for his team and his sponsor.

You and I can't hold autograph sessions to sign ticket stubs or caps like drivers do for their sponsors. But we can be available to answer people's questions about why we have faith in God. We represent him all the time through personal appearances – at home, school, work and even online.

Choose one thing you can do today to be an ambassador for God. Here are a few ideas to get you started:

* Say "God bless you" (instead of just "bless you") when someone sneezes.

* Smile, look people in the eye and be courteous as you interact with them.

* Always be ready to tell people the source of your joy if they ask.

* Write down Bible verses that offer comfort or cheer and keep them in your purse to hand out to anyone who seems sad or discouraged. (Isaiah 41:10, Psalm 31:24, Psalm 46:1, Matthew 11:28)

* When someone shares what is going wrong in her life, tell her you will pray for her. If you know her address, send her a card or e-mail to let you know you've been praying.

#23
Catching the Draft

Two are better than one, because they have a good return for
their work:
If one falls down, his friend can help him up.
Ecclesiastes 4:9-10a

Don't you love watching races at superspeedways when everyone is catching the draft? The fact that two or more cars running nose-to-tail can go faster by sticking together fascinates me.

I always knew drafting had something to do with aerodynamics – how the car interacts with the air as it speeds around the track. But I didn't completely grasp it until my son chose drafting for his sixth grade science project. Together we studied lift and drag and downforce until he understood it well enough to explain drafting to his classmates in an oral report.

When two cars are drafting, it appears that the second car is pushing the first one. But in reality, the opposite is true. As the lead car speeds along, it displaces the air in front of it and creates a vacuum behind its rear end. That vacuum effect actually draws the second car closer, thereby pulling it along.

If a driver loses the draft because his current drafting partner moves over to draft with someone else, it's called "getting hung out to dry." Because he is driving solo, the car no longer has extra speed and will drift back in traffic as the drafting cars zoom ahead. Sometimes the race commentators even say that a driver who has shifted to a line by himself can't find a friend.

Drafting often works like friendships. Not only do drafting partners hang together like buddies, they're actually working jointly to create an aerodynamic advantage that benefits both of them. Like drafting buddies, friends come alongside each other during struggles, encourage each other and pull each other up.

Ecclesiastes 4:9 describes both drafting and friendship: "Two are better than one, because they have a good return for their work."

Just like drivers depend on various drafting buddies during one race, we need diverse friendships throughout our lives. We have acquaintances that we recognize and greet when the opportunity is there. For a driver, an acquaintance might be the guy in the next pit stall. The two crew chiefs work together to coordinate pit stops to make it easier for both drivers to enter and exit their pit boxes without mishaps.

Then there are time-and-place friends, like the moms of your kids' soccer teammates or coworkers at the office. You are drawn together because circumstances give you common experiences. For a driver, these are the guys around him in the pack at any given moment. They share that part of the track and may become drafting partners if the opportunity presents itself.

The deepest friendships are with tried-and-true friends. They're the dear ones who stick with you through difficult times and love you no matter what is happening in your life. Often they are women you knew from childhood or through family connections. Drivers have this kind of friends, too — their teammates. These guys spend time in each other's race shops during the week, share information about engines and set-ups and are most likely to give each other a push at the finish line.

The best friends in my life are teammates in a way – we're sisters in Christ. We pray for each other, cheer each other to success and pick each other up when we fall. We stick together in our drafting line, not allowing anyone to get shuffled back in traffic all alone. I bet you have friends like that, too, taking turns blessing each other as life's drafting lines ebb and flow. Catching the draft is what racing – and life – is all about!

Prayer: Dear Lord, thank you for friends who are like drafting partners in my life. Help me to see when my friends need a hand and to accept help when they offer it. In Jesus' name, Amen.

Pit Stop

It's time to do some drafting in real life. Is there a friend you've lost track of because you're running at different places on the track? Someone from high school or college or your old neighborhood? Maybe it's time to draw closer to that friend and catch up. If she's far away, give her a call so you can hear each other's voices. If she's local, go for a manicure together and chat as your nails are beautified. Maybe go shopping or out to lunch. Or just have her over for coffee or tea or a mineral water. It doesn't matter what you do, just do something to link up and get your friendship back up to speed. It feels so good to reconnect, doesn't it?

#24
Daughter of the King

*I have loved you with an everlasting love; I have drawn you
with loving-kindness.*
Jeremiah 31:3

When I was a little girl, my dad coached his high school wrestling team to a record of 278 wins and 11 losses. Dad's team won the county championship 13 times in the 19 years he coached. When I observed how much respect the wrestlers, fans and other coaches had for my dad, I felt special because my dad was someone important.

Dad was inducted into several sports halls of fame. At one of the dinner ceremonies, Richard Petty was in attendance and Dad had the privilege of meeting him. My dad and Richard Petty - two guys with 200 career wins, two dads of daughters.

Did you know that in addition to son, Kyle, Richard Petty also has three daughters? I wonder if they ever dressed up as princesses when they were little girls. After all, since their dad is called "The King," each of them could rightly be called a princess.

Every little girl wants her daddy to see her as a princess. A girl benefits emotionally from a father's attention – being told she is talented and special and loved. But not every girl grows up with a loving daddy. Sadly, it is possible for a woman to reach adulthood never having heard the words, "I love you" from a father.

On top of that, as girls and women, we tend to judge ourselves harshly. From a tender age, we are bombarded with images of air-brushed models with smooth skin, sleek bodies and shiny hair. If we see wrinkles, bulges or not-so-perfect hair in the bathroom mirror, we don't feel beautiful or special. But that is the world's mirror, not God's.

God is not cold and distant. He does not judge you by your physical appearance. He created you. When a potter crafts a vase on his wheel, then glazes it and fires it in his kiln, it is his unique creation. Even if it has an imperfect shape or the finish has an unusual tint, he delights in his work of art.

My dear friend, you are a work of art created by God. You are special because your Heavenly Father is someone important and you are formed in His image. He loves you more than you can possibly imagine. It isn't only Richard Petty's girls who are "daughters of the King." You are a daughter of the King, too. In fact, you're a daughter of the King of Kings!

Whether you realize it or not, your Heavenly Father adores you. Song of Solomon 2:4 says "His banner over me is love." Imagine God waving a checkered flag over you and announcing, "This is my beloved daughter!"

Imagine the Lord enfolding you in His arms. You are His. He loves you so much He was willing to die for you. Wow, that's true love. Believe it. Celebrate it.

Prayer: Dear Lord, You really are my Father in heaven and I'm so glad You love me, even when I don't feel lovable or special. Thank you for showing that love by sending Jesus to wipe out my sins so I can be with You forever in heaven someday. In Jesus' name, Amen.

Pit Stop

We all have days when we feel unloved, unappreciated or unbeautiful. On those days, we need the truth of God's word to remind us who we are – well-loved daughters of the King! Grab some index cards and jot down the verses below about God's love for you. Keep them in your purse or post them on the mirror as a reminder.

Though the mountains be shaken and the hills be removed, yet my unfailing love for you will not be shaken nor my covenant of peace be removed," says the LORD, who has compassion on you. (Isaiah 54:10)

And I pray that you, being rooted and established in love, may have power ... to grasp how wide and long and high and deep is the love of Christ, and to know this love that surpasses knowledge—that you may be filled to the measure of all the fullness of God. (Ephesians 3:17b-19)

Listen, O daughter, consider and give ear: ...The king is enthralled by your beauty; honor him, for he is your lord. (Psalm 45:10a, 11)

His banner over me is love. (Song of Solomon 2:4b)

I have loved you with an everlasting love; I have drawn you with loving-kindness. (Jeremiah 31:3)

And so we know and rely on the love God has for us. God

is love. Whoever lives in love lives in God, and God in him. (I John 4:16)

The Lord your God is with you, he is mighty to save. He will take great delight in you, he will quiet you with his love, he will rejoice over you with singing. (Zephaniah 3:17)

#25
Going the Distance

In the morning, O Lord, you hear my voice;
in the morning I lay my requests before you and wait in
expectation.
Psalm 5:3

When I first heard the terms "qualifying trim" and "race trim," I had no idea what they meant. Now I know that for most races, the car is set up differently for qualifying than for the actual race. That's because the goals of qualifying and racing are very different.

The faster a driver runs his qualifying lap, the closer to the front he starts in the race lineup. So for qualifying, the team has one goal: get the fastest possible lap out of the car. A qualifying set-up has lots of tape on the front grille so air travels over the car, improving the aerodynamics. Teams can put less fuel in the car, use different shock absorbers and adjust the weight distribution to make it fly. Qualifying is about a short-term burst of speed.

On the other hand, a race set-up is about longevity. The goal is to have a car that handles well on long runs and goes fast for the entire race. Less tape is used on the grille so air can blow through and cool the engine. Hoses and fans are added to keep the brake system from overheating, too. Teams adjust the weight distribution and use shock absorbers that can go the distance.

Entering an actual race in qualifying trim would be futile. The car would run fast for a few laps, then the engine would start to overheat from all the grille tape, the shocks would give out and the handling would go away. It's like skipping breakfast - you zip out the door faster, but pretty soon your energy is sapped.

Life is more like a long race than a couple of qualifying laps. You have people to care for, errands to run, meals to make, phone calls, e-mails and a whole slew of other tasks to accomplish. There is an adjustment you can make each day that will prepare you to go the distance. It's a key part of your race trim called prayer.

Oftentimes we treat prayer like part of qualifying trim. We shoot up a short, quick request to God and zoom into our day. Later in the day, things start to overheat and fall apart as we succumb to fatigue or frustration.

Like putting race trim on a car, prayer takes time and commitment. But prayer is the most powerful tool in a believer's war wagon. Having intentional dialogue with the Lord each morning helps prepare our hearts for the day. We can worship Him, thank Him and ask Him for help. Sharing our problems and listening for His wisdom gives us strength to face the day.

Prayer, like race trim, gives you stamina to go the distance. Are you ready for today's race?

Prayer: Dear God, I want to spend time with you praying and listening for your voice. Help me to carve out time early each day to share my heart and seek your answers. In Jesus name, Amen.

Pit Stop

Race teams plan carefully so they have the right tools and enough time to put on race trim. Having a special prayer time takes a little planning, too.

Here are three things you can do ahead of time to make arrangements for your time with God.

1) Choose a "prayer closet." Find a spot that is private and without distractions.

2) Pick a time that works for most days. Morning is preferable if you can swing it.

3) Gather your tools: a Bible, pen and prayer journal.

Some women get up a bit earlier than the rest of the family to take advantage of the quietness. Try it. You might be surprised how much you look forward to your appointment with God.

#26
Cheering Them On

Therefore encourage one another and build each other up,
just as in fact you are doing.
1 Thessalonians 5:11

Okay, I admit it - I'm a fan of my favorite driver on his Facebook page. I get a kick out of the things he posts. Even more interesting are the responses of his many, many fans. When he posts something about how well his car handled in practice or how bummed he is about his finish, people type all kinds of encouragement. Whether his posts are positive or negative, people still rally behind him with uplifting, "go-get-'em, we love you, you're the best" comments.

As race fans, we are encouragers. We show support for our drivers by buying race tickets and merchandise, joining fan clubs and rooting for them in our living rooms. Now granted, the drivers don't see everything we fans do to show our team loyalty. But if my driver actually reads the responses he gets on Facebook, he should feel mightily encouraged.

The neat thing about receiving encouragement is that it strengthens us and buoys us up. Sometimes encouragement at just the right time gives the recipient a surge of determination to get the job done. That's what a crew chief counts on when he gives his driver a pep talk during a race. On the last few laps when his driver is leading, the crew chief might cheer, "Your lap times are the fastest. You're the man!"

Drivers' families encourage them, too. In interviews, Jimmie Johnson credits his wife, Chandra, with being behind his success, saying he couldn't do what he does without her. Jeff Gordon talks about his daughter, Ella, cheering him on with, "Go, Papa, go!"

Do you know someone who always makes you feel good by saying something positive? People who are "natural encouragers" bring sunshine into a room when they enter. They know enough about the lives of other so they can offer specific encouragement with ease.

If you're thinking, "that's not me, I tend to see the negatives," you're not alone. Many of us have a critical eye for finding things that need to be fixed instead of seeing the genuine efforts others are making. How can we stop nitpicking and become encouragers?

It starts in our head, because thoughts are the seeds of spoken words. We must start by taking captive our critical thoughts and looking for good intentions in others so that we can make encouraging comments. According to Proverbs 18:21, our words can have the power of life and death. Yikes! I want to speak life-giving words, don't you?

Imagine a flower in a pot representing a person you can encourage. If bountiful showers of encouragement fall, the flower flourishes and blooms to its full potential. If there are a few raindrops of support here and there, the leaves wither and petals wilt, but it hangs on. If there is not one drop of appreciation or applause, the flower dries up.

People are just like that flower. Think about how a positive comment from you changes your child or husband - a wilting face transforms into a radiant one! As a woman and mom, you set the tone in your home. It can be a place of perceived rejection, where support and encouragement are sparse. Or it can be a haven of mutual inspiration, where you rally to cheer each other's efforts. Which will you choose?

Prayer: Dear God, help me to find opportunities to encourage my loved ones with affirming words. Please give me spiritual eyes to see their good intentions and a tongue that is quick to bless their efforts with praise. In Jesus' name, Amen.

Pit Stop

It's easy to rally behind our favorite drivers on Sundays. But our families deserve our support and cheering all week long. I want to be my family's biggest fan, too.

Here's an idea to get you started on blessing your husband, kids, friends or whoever else with verbal encouragement. Grab a notebook and put each person's name at the top of a separate page. Under each name, make a list of specific things you can say to encourage that person. For each person, make a list of activities, interests and chores as a starting point for finding things to applaud.

For instance, if your child plays soccer, point out something good he or she did on the field. Give a shout out to your teenager who displayed patience or loyalty. Tell your husband how much you appreciate the yard work he did.

For those of you who are natural encouragers, making a list may sound silly. But for people like me who tend to be on the critical side, thinking ahead is helpful.

Good ways to start your comments are:

"I appreciate that you..."

"I liked it when you..."

"You are doing such a good job with..."

As you practice verbally building up your loved ones, it becomes easier and more natural. Your example may even inspire them to encourage others. Go, family, go!

#27
Brakes, Bodies and Breakdowns

Do you not know that your body is a temple of the Holy Spirit, who is in you,
whom you have received from God? You are not your own;
you were bought at a price.
Therefore honor God with your body.
I Corinthians 6:19-20

Even though the accelerator is a stock car driver's best friend, his brakes play a key role in racing, too. The tighter the turns in an oval track, the more often a driver has to brake to keep the car from flying into the wall. That's why short track racing can stress the brakes, causing them to heat up and potentially give out. To get ready for tracks like Bristol and Martinsville, mechanics use thicker brake pads and sturdier brake parts on the cars.

The more often and harder a driver hits the brakes, the more strain on the brakes. Heat from the rotors can change the handling of the car and build tire pressure. Sometimes the searing heat melts the rubber around steel beads in the rim of the tire and air leaks out. Either way, the tire goes down, sending the car into the wall - not fun for the driver or team.

You can see the brake rotors glowing red during short track races, which means their temperature is 1200-1300 degrees. Brake pad temperatures go even higher. Cars have fans blowing air on the brakes to cool them, but sometimes it's not enough to keep them from overheating.

When working with machines, there is a delicate balance

between maximizing performance and avoiding breakdown. No crew chief or mechanic wants to stress an engine or other car part to the point that it malfunctions and ruins the car's performance. It's frustrating for a team to work on a car all week and end up with a DNF.

Sometimes an engine blows up with no warning - smoke billows from the car and it's over. But other times subtle warning signs show up when something is amiss. The driver feels a vibration. Water temperature starts to rise. The engine sounds peculiar.

Like cars, our human bodies have limits to how much stress they can take before problems surface. When our bodies are over-stressed, they give us warning signs like headaches, digestive issues, high blood pressure, sleeping problems and achy joints.

Mechanics take precautions to prevent break wear and damage, like using thicker brake pads. What can we do to defend our health and protect our bodies from harm? You already know, but here it is anyway: Eat nutritious foods, but not too much. Drink enough water. Exercise. Get 7-8 hours of sleep each night. Laugh often. Wear your seat belt. You can probably think of a few more. Most of us know the drill, but we still don't take care of ourselves all the time.

Race car drivers are fortunate because tires can be changed and a blown engine can be rebuilt. But each of us only gets one body for our life's race. In order to honor God, we need to treat our bodies well. What can you do today to relieve stress and take care of your body?

Prayer: Dear God, thank you for this amazing body you have given me. Help me to be disciplined to take precautions to keep my body healthy and strong so that I can serve and honor You. In Jesus' name, Amen.

Pit Stop

How can drivers use their brakes as much as they need to at short tracks while preventing brake problems that cause blowouts? If you knew the answer to that question, crew chiefs would line up to talk to you!

We can follow good eating, exercise and sleep habits to stay healthy. But there are other fun things that help relieve stress, too. Laughter, for instance. Do you remember the last time you had an out-of-control, tears-rolling-down-your-cheeks belly laugh? Watch comedy movies and read humorous books to fill your mind with light, uplifting humor. Tickling the funny bone makes you feel good.

Play sports that you enjoy for fun and exercise – tennis, golf, swimming, whatever. Something you can do at home with no sports equipment is dancing. Turn on your favorite music and dance around the house to your heart's content. Goodbye stress, hello dance floor!

#28
Colors

*Whenever I bring clouds over the earth and the rainbow
appears in the clouds, I will remember my covenant between
me and you and all living creatures of every kind.
Never again will the waters become a flood to destroy all life*
Genesis 9:14-15

Racing is a colorful sport. With football, baseball and other team sports, each side has two colors, so the stadium is filled with jerseys and hats in those few colors. But at a race track, every color of the rainbow is represented.

The colors people wear tell us a lot about who they are. A sea of orange in the stands might mean a group of Joey Logano fans. A mixture of colors might mean divided loyalties, like in my family. My husband likes Dale Earnhardt, Jr. I follow Kasey Kahne. Our older son is a Jeff Gordon fan and our younger son likes Tony Stewart. We make a multi-colored, motley crew on race day, each wearing our favorite driver's t-shirt and cap.

In the garage and on pit road, it's easy to tell which team a crew member works for by his fire suit colors. Once in a while teams throw us for a loop by suiting up in different colors, like when an associate sponsor name is on the hood.

Colors help us find our favorite driver when he's flying by on the television screen. Drivers use colors to zero in on their pit stalls on pit road. Paint scheme colors also help drivers know who is approaching in the rearview mirror.

The flags of NASCAR are color-coded like traffic lights -

green for go, yellow for caution and red for stop. There's the black flag telling him to get off the track that no driver wants to see. On the other hand, the one-lap-to-go white flag is a welcome sight to the race leader. The only thing better is the checkered flag signaling the end of the race. You're the winner – woo hoo! In recent years, the addition of the green-and-white checkered flags has made the end of races more exciting by adding laps to prevent a finish under caution.

Would it be as enjoyable to watch a race in black and white? No way. The only thing that would look right would be the checkered flag!

Colors are a gift from God that make life interesting and give nature its signature beauty. He created such an amazing variety of shades for us to enjoy. Just as the racing flags have meaning and may invoke a certain emotion in us, the splendor of nature affects us, too. When we see a purple-blue cornflower by the side of the road or the orange sun dancing through charcoal shadows of trees, we can't help but think of the One who created it all.

God used colors to make a covenant with all the people and critters on the earth. His rainbow signifies his promise to never flood the whole earth again. Every time I see a rainbow, it reminds me of God's creativity and faithfulness. Beautiful colors are all around you - make it a point to enjoy some of them today.

Prayer: Dear God, you are the master artist with the whole earth as your canvas. Thank you for the gift of colors, from muted pastels to bright shades to deep earth tones. Help me to take time to appreciate your handiwork. In Jesus name, Amen.

Pit Stop

Colors can enrich our lives in all kinds of ways. Here are two ideas to put a spring in your step and a glow in your cheeks.

First, get outside! Spend a few moments watching birds, looking at flowers or gazing up at the sky or clouds. No matter where you live or what the weather, the beauty of nature is waiting for you to discover it. Breathe deeply and praise God for the glorious intricacies of the natural world.

Second, open your closet. Go through your clothing and get rid of clothing in colors that make you look washed out. Why wear stuff that doesn't compliment you? Keep blouses and tops in colors that bring out the best in your eyes and complexion. Color yourself beautiful!

#29
Is Your Sleep Tank Full?

Then, because so many people were coming and going...he said to them,
"Come with me by yourselves to a quiet place and get some rest."
Mark 6:31

Yesterday was a stressful day. First, somebody hurt my feelings in a big way. Next, I discovered a major project for work had to be revamped and taken in a different direction. Later I spent three straight hours online with a computer software technician who helped me fix a computer problem. Most days I'm pretty upbeat, but that triple play of events left me frustrated and exhausted.

Today is a new day. My balanced viewpoint is back. I'm reassessing the work project, getting organized and tackling it head on. I'm grateful that my computer issue is fixed.

What made the difference in my outlook? I filled up my sleep tank. A good night's sleep rejuvenated me, which made everything look better. There are many worse things in life than muddled work projects and computer glitches. But because I was chronically sleep-deprived when those problems occurred, they seemed like disasters. Being refreshed by sleep gave me a softened, more rational perspective on yesterday's events.

Restorative sleep is such a blessing. But it's easy to get in the habit of staying up late to get things done. By cheating ourselves out of sleep day after day, many of us become chronically sleep-deprived, which can affect our physical and mental health.

Missing your beauty sleep can cause all kinds of troubles, big and small: irritability, blurry vision, slower reaction time, decreased concentration and memory. Plus, being tired feels miserable. Experts say chronic lack of sleep may even contribute to serious health conditions like high blood pressure and heart disease.

I wonder if race car drivers ever suit up and strap in when their sleep tanks are empty. Many drivers were blessed with new babies in the past few years. Do those new dads ever lose sleep because the baby is colicky during the night before a race?

Even without crying babies, drivers might have trouble sleeping sometimes. Think about the repercussions of a sleep-deprived guy racing at high speeds: slower reaction time, poor concentration, blurry vision. Yikes! Add in the likelihood of getting frustrated more quickly and you have a recipe for wrecking. Race car drivers cannot afford to be exhausted behind the wheel - and neither can you.

Have you ever had a day that knocked you flat and made you feel like crawling into bed and covering your head? That bed might be just what you need! Instead of stewing about a problem, try sleeping on it. God provided nighttime because He knew our human bodies need to rest frequently.

Don't let your sleep tank run dry. To keep a clear mind and a balanced perspective, make sleep a priority.

Prayer: Dear God, thank you for the gift of rest which restores my body and mind. Please show me where to change my schedule to make adequate sleep a priority. In Jesus name, Amen.

Pit Stop

How can you fill up your sleep tank? Here are two ideas to try.

First, add several hours per week to your sleep tank by doing bedtime preparations earlier. For example, each night I pack lunchboxes, put the dog in her crate, shut down the computer, brush my teeth and lock all the doors. By completing these tasks by 9:30, instead of 10:00, I can hit the sack earlier. Could you do bedtime stuff earlier in the evening, so you're not scrambling at the last minute?

Second, try an experiment. Every night for an entire week, sleep for eight hours. If you have to go to bed earlier to make it work, do it. At the end of the week, assess how you feel physically and emotionally while running on a full sleep tank.

#30
Pit Stop for the Soul

"Martha, Martha," the Lord answered, "You are worried and upset about many things, but only one thing is needed. Mary has chosen what is better, and it will not be taken away from her."
Luke 10:41-42

Remember Mary and Martha from the Bible? When Jesus came to dinner at their home, Martha wanted everything to be perfect. She scurried about, performing last-minute household chores while guests were arriving. She mopped her brow and wrung her hands, hoping she could get everything done in time for her guests to enjoy a nice meal.

Do you ever feel like Martha, that there's so much work to be done and not enough time to do it? I sure do! Each day feels like a race to accomplish many tasks. I feel like I'm speeding forward, eyes focused straight ahead, hands gripping the wheel, accelerator pushed to the floor - trying to cover as much ground as I can in as little time as possible. When I'm efficient, organized and "in the zone," I make good progress and avoid dumb mistakes like exchanging paint with my fellow racers. Other days I spin my tires on restarts, waste time serving pass-through penalties and never really get much accomplished.

Why do some days feel like Victory Lane and others like a DNF? For me, often the difference is whether or not I spend a few moments with Jesus. Sitting quietly with the Lord is like taking a pit stop for your soul.

Pit stops don't take much time, but they make a big impact

for the driver and his race. Let's say the race is four hours long and a driver has six or seven pit stops totaling about one or two minutes seconds. So the team used a couple minutes out of four hours to refuel, put on new tires and make adjustments on the car. In that short time, the pit crew made changes that could totally alter the rest of the race.

I imagine poor, stressed Martha didn't take time for rest on the day Jesus came to dinner. So when she noticed her sister, Mary, sitting at the feet of Jesus instead of helping her in the kitchen, Martha flipped out. She griped to Jesus that Mary wasn't helping her. But Jesus said that Mary had made the better choice. Sitting with Him was better than basting the roast lamb again or throwing an extra loaf of bread in the oven.

Martha raced and raced, working without resting. Mary knew when it was time to make a pit stop. Jesus knew that we can become resentful and empty if we forget to take time for refreshment and rest. He wanted Martha to take a break and refuel herself. Jesus wanted Martha to make a pit stop!

How much time does a pit stop take? Comparatively speaking, one or two minutes of pitting out of four hours of racing is about the same as ten minutes out of a 24-hour day. What if you took ten minutes today and used it for a personal pit stop to sit at the feet of Jesus? Take your foot off the accelerator, coast to pit road speed and feel your racing heart begin to calm. Listen quietly for His voice in the stillness. As you focus on how much He loves and cares for you, allow Him to fill you with strength, joy and peace.

Prayer: Dear God, please speak to me today as I sit at your feet. Maximize my time and energy for this day so that I can accomplish the work you have set before me. In Jesus' name, Amen.

Pit Stop

For many women, it's hard to just sit still. We're so used to being busy. Will you try making a ten-minute pit stop?

Find a quiet place where you are comfortable and there is good lighting. For your ten-minute pit stop, try Mary's kind of busyness instead of Martha's. Busy your hands by cradling your Bible. Busy your eyes and heart by searching the scriptures. Busy your lips with prayer. Then, take a deep breath...and busy your ears with listening for the voice of Jesus.

#31
The Final Lap

Greater love has no one than this,
that he lay down his life for his friends.
John 15:12

Before I was a NASCAR fan, I wondered how people could spend hours watching cars driving in circles. There just wasn't any appeal for me. But when our older son developed an interest in stock car racing, we tuned in for the first points race of the season.

I was captivated by the camaraderie between the announcers who called the race. From the stories and observations they related, the commentators seemed to know the drivers personally, and spoke about them as if they were old friends. Some drivers had their wives alongside them for the opening ceremony. Pit crew guys formed lines and slapped hands and everyone bowed their heads to pray together. It seemed like the NASCAR folks were one big happy family.

As I watched, it became apparent that one announcer, Darrell Waltrip, was the older brother of Michael Waltrip, who was driving in the race. There were other sets of brothers, too – Rusty, Kenny and Mike Wallace, Terry and Bobby Labonte, Ward and Jeff Burton. And there was a father and son pair on the track, too – Dale Earnhardt, Sr. and Dale Earnhardt, Jr.

One of these racing families, and indeed all of motorsports was changed forever by the time this race ended. It was the first race I ever watched, but the last ride for racing legend Dale Earnhardt, Sr. He was killed instantly when his car hit the outside wall in turn four of the final lap. A split-second later his teammate Michael Waltrip and son, Dale Earnhardt, Jr. crossed the finish line in first and second place, respectively.

Race fans will never forget Dale Earnhardt, Sr. There's probably not a fan alive who doesn't recognize his face and the paint scheme of his #3 car. My doctor's four-year-old son has never been to a race, yet somehow he knows. While playing with his toy stock cars he told her, "Mommy, Dale Earnhardt, Junior's daddy crashed and he's in heaven." Even a young fan who wasn't born when he died knows about him.

Perhaps losing Dale Earnhardt, Sr. helped save the lives of other drivers. After his tragic accident, changes in safety equipment and track structure were made. The following year, the HANS device (Head And Neck Support) was mandated for all drivers. Later, race tracks altered the construction of many inside and outside walls, installing the "SAFER" barriers. These "Steel And Foam Energy Reduction" walls absorb more of the impact in a crash, decreasing chances of driver injuries.

Did Dale Earnhardt, Sr. lay down his life for the protection of his friends? Of course not! But there is one person who did – Jesus Christ. He died so that every person can be forgiven of their sins. Those who believe in Jesus as their Savior have the assurance of seeing each other again in heaven someday.

Unfortunately, loss is a part of life for every family. Each one of us will have a final lap in this life. What a comfort to know the separation of death doesn't have to last forever. Will your family be reunited someday in heaven? There is only one way to be sure – by trusting Jesus as Lord of your life.

Race Fans' Devotions to Go

Prayer – Dear God, thank you that I can be assured of being in heaven when I leave this earth simply by trusting in Jesus as my Savior. Amen.

Pit Stop

Talk to your loved ones about their beliefs. If you or your family members need some support, ask a pastor for help. If you are already a believer and some family members are not, tell them how much you want to be with them in heaven. Explain how they can have that assurance and lead them in a prayer to accept Jesus as their Savior if they are willing.

Race Fans' Devotions to Go